I AM
Creating My
Own Success

by
Barry Thomas Bechta

**UNCONDITIONAL
LOVE BOOKS**

*Redefining, Guiding, and Inspiring Humanity's
Connection to the Creative Power within.*

I AM Creating My Own Success
by
Barry Thomas Bechta

Library and Archives Canada Cataloguing in Publication

Bechta, Barry Thomas, 1968-
  I am creating my own success / by Barry Thomas Bechta.

ISBN 978-0-9686835-5-2

  1. Success--Religious aspects.
2. Self-realization--Religious aspects.
3. Spiritual life. I. Title.

BL65.S84B42 2009   204   C2009-905909-6

Publisher's Note

This publication is designed to provide accurate and authoritative information in regard to the subject matter covered. It is sold with the understanding that the author/publisher is not engaged in rendering psychological, legal, or other professional service. If advice or other assistance is required in those areas, the services of a competent professional should be sought.

I AM
Creating My
Own Success

I AM Choice.
AM I Choosing This Consciously?
I AM Accessing This from God's Limitless
Potential. I AM Declaring This into Being.
Thank You God.

ACKNOWLEDGEMENTS

GOD

Ellen and Clare

Binah, Anthony, and Zac

Stephen, Margaret, Gabe, and Sam

Melinda, Paul, Sydney, and Gryphon

Everyone whom has ever been a part of my life

Everyone whom has ever helped me to be more in my life

I Thank God for each and everyone of your loving hearts.

TO THE READER

I AM Choosing everything I AM experiencing. I Choose Consciously because I know I AM the Creator of my experience. Every Choice I make leads to another experience. My Choices manifest whether I AM Conscious or unconscious about them. Whether I believe I can accomplish something or I doubt I can, my Choices manifest to prove my beliefs. My Intentions within my Choices Create My experiences.

My journey to Being a Successful Conscious Pilot in my life has taken the perfect amount of time for me. Everyone on the journey towards spiritual awareness and self actualization takes the perfect amount of time for them to access and open themselves to Choose and Accept more Love, Success, and Abundance into their life. We are all here to realize and actualize who and what we Choose to Be.

Some of the things I experience seem to BE the exact opposite of what I Desire to experience, however ALL my experiences are there for me to Consciously Choose Who and What I Desire to BE. When I heal my beliefs in separation from All That Is, I Create Unity with All That Is.

My entire Being Declares my deepest heartfelt most secret beliefs about my life and myself. My Declarations, about Who and What I AM, are expressed through all my thoughts, feelings, words, and actions. Every Declaration I Choose puts the entire Universe in motion to Create my experience of my announcements. Everything I Decide and Declare I AM.

I Can Choose Only One thing at a time. Either I Choose a firm belief in Love, Life, and God or I Choose my fear (feelings eroding away reality) to affect my Choices. Love is an expression of my unfailing belief in my Success. My Success or lack of Success is always and only my Responsibility.

Whatever I Choose through my unified Heart, Mind, and Being by using all my thoughts, feelings, words, and actions Manifests without fail.

God is Love, Success, and Abundance forming limitlessly into All That Is. My Choices allow me to experience my deepest heartfelt most secret beliefs by accessing them within All That Is. God is Limitless Potential. I AM Limitless Choice. Whatever I

Choose, God Manifests.

When I experience something once, it can be By Chance or My Choice. When I experience something twice, it can be By Accident or My Coincidence. When I experience something three times or more, it can be My Bad Habits or My Success Habits. When I Choose something Consciously and Consistently I AM Creating my Own Success on purpose.

Choose and Declare Successfully from the Limitless Potential,
Barry Thomas Bechta

TABLE OF CONTENTS

I AM CHOICE   Page 1

I AM THOUGHTS   Page 7

I AM FEELINGS   Page 13

I AM WORDS   Page 19

I AM ACTIONS   Page 23

I AM HEART   Page 29

I AM MIND   Page 35

I AM BEING   Page 41

I AM EXPERIENCE   Page 45

I AM SUCCESS   Page 51

I AM LASTING FREEDOM   Page 55

AFFIRMATIONS FOR MY SUCCESS   Page 59

I AM Choice

I Choose everything in my experience
I Choose being fear or Being Faith
I Choose being in pain or Being In Joy
I Choose being poor or Being Abundant
I Choose being illusions or Being Dreams
I Choose being normal or Being Miracles
I Choose being unconscious or Being Conscious
I Choose being worries or Being Confidence
I Choose being separate or Being Unity
I Choose being absent or Being Present
I Choose being human or Being God

It is always my Choice

I AM CHOICE

I Choose everything in my experience

I Choose absolutely everything in my experience. Everything is a result of my thoughts, feelings, words, and actions. Through my life, I have been both aware and unaware of this truth.

At the heart of this truth is God. God is All. I AM One within God. God is All within me. When I forget this truth my experience can be a struggle. When I Choose this truth my experience flows effortlessly and easily.

No matter what I experience, I have Chosen it. I have Chosen it through all my thoughts, feelings, words, and actions. My thoughts, feelings, words, and actions are the Creative tools God provides to All That Is.

When I use my thoughts, feelings, words, and actions incongruently, I Create my experience incongruently. I still Create my experience, yet my incongruent messages send many different requests to the Universe.

I can paint a house with four cans of different coloured paints or four cans of the same coloured paint. They both Create the result of a painted house. Do I enjoy the way my house looks?

When I use my thoughts, feelings, words, and actions congruently I Create my experience powerfully. I Paint my house and my world harmoniously. I flow with life rather than struggle against life.

My Intentions within my Choices Create My experiences. God, Love, and Life provide me with constant feedback corresponding to my Choices. God, Love, and Life give me immediate directions toward Creating the Life of my Dreams. My feelings of Joy always in all ways reminds me that I AM on track.

I Choose being fear or Being Faith

God, Love, and Life wish wholeheartedly for me to experience a life of Ease and Flow; a life of Quality and Quantity;

a life of Love, Success, and Abundance. To help me achieve that end, God, Love, and Life provides me with constant feedback and immediate directions to Create the Life of my dreams. When I access God's Joy my life takes off in beautiful ways.

This powerful flow in my life occurs either fearfully or Faithfully. It is my Choice. It is easier and more fun to be Faithful in the journey. Whenever I recognize and acknowledge that I have been affected by fear, I can quickly access my Faith again.

I Choose being in pain or Being In Joy.

God, Love, and Life is All That Is. All That Is guides me to be open to the process of life. This process takes different paths. When the path goes slowly, it is a struggle and tiresome work. When the path flows, it is effortless and easy. All paths are imbued with guidance when I AM Open to the possibilities presented before me.

All paths encourage me to release the struggle and Relax into the Joy and Flow of life. I may imagine that the way to my fulfilment is only along the path of struggle, however it is more easily reached along the path of Joy and Flow. Both paths lead to the same destination, however one is filled with pain and fear, while the other is filled with Joy and Faith.

God supports me, no matter what I Choose, and God guides me to experience more Ease and Success. Whether I Choose being fear or Being Faith, I AM Supported in all my Choices. I Can Choose being in pain or Being In Joy, and God supports my journey no matter what I Choose.

I Choose being poor or Being Abundant

I Choose everything. I Choose being poor or Being Abundant. I Choose being illusions or Being Dreams. Whatever I focus upon, I place my Creative energy into. My thoughts, feelings, words, and actions powerfully set my Creation Vibration.

The Universe is Abundant. With the right focus as to what

I perceive, I can Open up to Abundance in every situation. It is my Choice. There is Only Abundance or there is a perception of Abundant lack.

I get to Choose whatever I decide. There is nothing stopping me in my Choice. My Choices are always Successful. I make Choices and my Intentions within my Choices Create my experiences. Some experiences match the results I envision and other match different visions. Always in all ways my Choices are Successful.

I Choose being illusions or Being Dreams

To manifest particular results, I Choose to use my thoughts, feelings, words, and actions congruently. To manifest perfect results, I Choose what I would like and flow with what I get. God, Love, and Life always provides the perfect people, places, or things directing me to where I Choose, no matter what appears to be.

When I struggle against the illusions in my outer world, I energize the illusions and they continue to manifest as my experience. When I flow and focus on my Dreams in my inner world, I energize them and they manifest as my experience.

I Choose being normal or Being Miracles

Seeing and Being are unified. I can Only see what I first can BE. When I AM being normal, I AM seeing normal. When I AM being Miracles, I AM seeing Miracles.

Everything I AM Being, I AM Choosing to Be. Everything I AM Seeing, I AM Choosing to Be; angry, depressed, fearful, Happy, Joyous, Faithful. I AM Choosing All That Is and whatever is Right Here Right Now I have chosen.

I Choose being unconscious or Being Conscious

When I AM being unconscious, I play a victim and

relinquish my Responsibility for All I AM. When I AM Being Conscious, I play a Creator and Accept Responsibility for All I AM.

Being Conscious is a simple Choice when I see it and Choose it. Every Choice is simple to make and simply Creates my Consequences. When I AM unhappy with the Consequences I AM experiencing, I can Choose differently.

I Choose being worries or Being Confidence

Whenever my Choices take a long time to manifest I can worry and accept to believe in the illusions of my outer experience or I can Choose Being Confidence in the Dreams of my inner experience.

All of my thoughts Create my reality. I Choose all of my thoughts. That is the Truth of my experience. I Choose it all. I Choose what I think. I Choose the way I feel. I Choose words that curse or words that praise. I Choose actions that erode or actions that build. I Choose this through my Beliefs and sometimes through beliefs in my worries.

I Choose being separate or Being Unity

In my entire experience, I Choose being separate from God, Love, and Life or Being Unity with All That Is. When I Choose being separate from God, Love, and Life, I Choose to remove myself from the Love, Success, and Abundance of the entire Universe.

When I Choose Being Unity with God, Love, and Life first and foremost, All That Is falls into place and provides me with All I AM. God can provide me with absolutely anything I can possibly imagine when I Unify completely with the Pure Potential of God/Life/Energy.

I Choose being absent or Being Present

I Choose whether I AM absent from or Present with God. Since God is The Source of absolutely everything, it is very counter productive to Choose being absent from All That Is.

In Choosing to Be Present, I also Choose to Unify with All That Is. Being Present with All That Is means I AM Choose Being One with All That Is. Being One with All That Is means I Choose Being Present with every experience whether I consider it good (works for me) or bad (works against me).

To judge something as bad means I have Chosen to be absent from the good Right Now being presented to me. Everything that is presented to me is good. When I AM Present, I easily recognise this truth.

I Choose being human or Being God

In every moment of Now, I can Only Be One thing. I Choose something in every moment. What I See is what I Choose to Be.

To Choose being human is to accept all of the limitations of being human. Being human, I may imagine it is impossible to Create the life of my dreams. Being human, I may accept a life of lack, limitation, and suffering. Being human being I may imagine I am separate from God.

When I Choose Being God, I AM One with God. I Choose living a spiritual experience through a human form. I experience all that being human is and all that Being God offers. It is my Choice.

I AM CHOICE

I AM Thoughts

My thoughts place my orders
My Choices Create my Consequences
Until I Control my Subconscious
My Subconscious can be in control
I Choose to be totally out of my mind
I Choose to program My Subconscious
With God's Love, Success, and Abundance
Fears and Worries are both illusions and prayers
They are illusions because they are only my thoughts
They are prayers because All my thoughts
access the Limitless Potential of God to
Create All my experiences

I AM Thoughtful

I AM THOUGHTS

The capacity of my thoughts is more magnificent, more impressive, and more powerful that I could ever imagine from a perspective of being human. Absolutely everything ever Created began with a thought. The entire Universe with all of its stars, planets, and galaxies all began as thoughts. Absolutely everything on Earth from trees to cars to roads to books began with thoughts.

My thoughts place my Choices

My thoughts go way beyond that. Absolutely everything in my experience is Created first with a thought generated by me. My thoughts are my Choices concerning the direction I wish to proceed in the experiences I envision.

My thoughts and Choices are my orders. I both eat in and work at the smorgasbord restaurant where God is the cook. Sometimes God is a short order cook and sometimes God is long order cook. Always God follows my direction. God can only do for me what God can do through me. My thoughts are the avenue through which God Manifests my experience.

My Choices Create my Consequences

My thoughts and Choices place my orders with God and without any effort on my part my orders Manifest. As long as I order one thing at a time and then order new things at different times, my orders are continually fulfilled.

Sometimes this process is uncanny and amazingly simple. I think of a song and it is the next one that plays on the radio. I think of calling a friend and the next phone call I receive is from that very friend. I place my order with God, move onto something else, and then my order manifests without any great effort on my part.

In my past, my orders have rarely Manifested directly. This happens for a number of reasons. A major reason the manifestation process is slow is that I keep going back to the kitchen and modifying the order that I already placed and as a result God starts the order over again. Everyone else in the restaurant seems to be eating their meal already, while I wait for mine to be prepared from scratch with each additional order modification.

Until I Control my Subconscious My Subconscious can be in control

Another major reason that my order is slow to arrive is that my subconscious placed the order for me. As I looked at the menu, I saw many glorious items; dream items. I Chose them and placed my order with God. God reads the order as it appears in my heart and God gets the fullest version as written by my subconscious.

My subconscious is a record of my deepest heartfelt most secret beliefs concerning all my dreams. Many times in my past, I have placed orders that were the exact opposite of my deepest heartfelt most secret beliefs about my Choices. God manifests the orders as they appear in my heart always in all ways. Nothing more and nothing less.

I Choose to be totally out of my mind

When I get out of my mind, I can feel what is in my heart. My heart can be full of my fears, worries, and nightmares, or full of my Hopes, Wishes, and Dreams. Each of these are thoughts that I have accepted as my truth within my Core at one time or another.

My deepest heartfelt most secret beliefs in my heart are different than the beliefs in my mind. The thoughts in my heart I have accepted and let go of. I may have even placed the order years ago without a single change up to this day. God effortlessly fulfills all my orders.

The thoughts in my mind are orders that I place with God/Life/Energy. In my past, I imagined that my worry and work could more effectively manifest what God Manifests without any effort required from me.

I Choose to program My Subconscious

When I take time to meditate and be quiet I can hear my heart. When I listen my heart tells me what my subconscious beliefs are. The more I listen to my heart, the more I discover than my subconscious is waiting for me to listen to my heart and allow the Manifesting power of Love it possesses to be set free. God/Life/Energy is ready to provide absolutely everything I dream and desire in my life when I acknowledge God's Presence and ask for God's help.

With God's Love, Success, and Abundance

Within my heart is the key to God's Love, Success, and Abundance. That key is accessed by going within and listening to my heart. The door is open. The offer is perpetual. The results are experiential. All that I could ever imagine is accessible within me and manifests through me when I Choose to accept my part in this process.

Fears and Worries are both illusions and prayers
They are illusions because they are only my thoughts
They are prayers because All my thoughts
access the Limitless Potential of God to
Create All my experiences

When my thoughts are filled with Faith and Confidence, I place my order with God and then don't even give it a second thought. I know it is going to manifest and it does. No questions asked. No effort on my part. There is Nothing to do. I AM Grateful in this easy part of my journey.

Fears and worries are illusions. They are my thoughts in anything other than God. They are worthless and they can Create a life of fears and worries when I Choose them. It is always my Choice what I think about.

Fears and worries are the major reason my manifestations take so long in my life. When I worry about how I will ever get the things I dream about, or I fear that they will never come. In effect, I go and place another order with God, a clear and certain request for more of the same, and God starts from scratch with each new order.

If my next order is for something different, then God now has two things to manifest. This is no problem for God and God actually likes fulfilling all of my orders. The more I choose with Faith and Confidence the more God provides quickly and easily. It is always my Choice what I Choose to think about.

I AM THOUGHTS

When I get out of my mind,
I can feel what is in my heart.

I AM Feelings

Sadness, Frustration, and Anxiety
Are Feelings that separate me from God
They become Depression, Anger, and Fear
When I forget my Oneness with God
God is found Only Now Here
God is No Where else
God is Present Presents Presence
Joy, Ease, and Relaxation
Are Feelings that amplify God
Into Love, Success, and Abundance
When I Accept All That Is Now Here

I AM Feelings

I AM FEELINGS

The Universe is as orderly as a machine. On the one hand, it is an immense photocopy machine that reproduces my thoughts as forms. On the other hand, the Universe is a large train of my dreams. Each train car is a single dream. The more dreams I have, the longer it takes for the train to reach its peak speed.

My feelings are the power energizing the Universal machine in my own life. The fuel I place in the Universal machine affects the results of this finely tuned machine. I can use anger and frustration to power this machine or the most Joyous fuel. My feelings Attract my experiences.

Sadness, Frustration, and Anxiety
Are Feelings that separate me from God
They become Depression, Anger, and Fear
When I forget my Oneness with God

When I focus on past pains, present problems, or future fears, I allow sadness, frustration, and anxiety to fuel my Universe. When I wish to change something in the past that went poorly, I can experience sadness. When I try to control a person, place, or thing in the present, I can experience frustration. When I worry incessantly about future possibilities, I can experience anxiety. All of these feelings intensify my feeling of separation from God, which sets my Creation Vibration and Attracts my experiences of my Vibrational Choices.

When I stay in a place of sadness, it eventually leads to depression; frustration leads to anger; anxiety leads to all out fear. When I feel depressed, angry, or fearful, I have completely forgotten that I AM One with God.

There is Only God. There is Only my experience of God. My Feelings power my experience of God. Any Feeling that separates me from my experience of God, also separates me from my power with God. God can Only be, what God can Be through me.

Feelings that separate me from God are there for me to accept. I accept them as a part of my experience by recognizing they fuel my experiences. When I use the same type of fuel, I get the same type of experiences. Once I accept separation Feelings as a part of my experience, I accept separation from God/Life/Energy. I Can Choose Feelings that Unify me with God/Life/Energy. I Choose to Accept What Is and then Choose where I AM Going.

When I discover that my Feelings are clouded and supporting separation from God, I am disappointed with my past, frustrated with other people, places, and things, or anxious about future possibilities that I empower with my very feelings to show up as I imagine.

God is found Only Now Here
God is No Where else
God is Present Presents Presence

God is All That Is. God is Only Now Here. God is Present Presents Presence. Any thing I perceive other than Present Presents Presence is Only an illusion of thought.

In my past only my memories of what was lives. In my future only dreams of what could be live. In my present there are either God's Gifts or my perceptions of problems. Problems are illusions I can buy into and fuel with my Feelings of frustration and anger. Or I can release my perceptions of problems and Choose to see that these are incredible Gifts Right Here Right Now.

God is All That Is. There is nothing else. When I discover that my Feelings are fuelled by anything other than Only God, I also discover that I have Chosen to deny God. When I Choose to deny God, I Choose to rely on everything other than God, which are only thoughts I have Chosen to believe are more powerful than All That Is.

Joy, Ease, and Relaxation
Are Feelings that amplify God

When I experience Joy, Ease, and Relaxation I AM One with God. God is totally Joyous, Easy, and Relaxed. God is Flowing and Growing. God Opens. God Loves. God Allows. God encourages the happiest possible results. God is full of pleasant surprises. God is wonderful.

Anything other than Joy, Ease, and Relaxation is a result of my denial of God. When I deny God, I resist whatever is Now Here. Whatever is in my experience Right Here Right Now is God reminding me to Choose Only God. That is easy some of the time and definitely satisfying every time I Choose Only God.

The sooner I accept What Is and find God's Gift in the Present Presents Presence, the sooner I grow together with God. Growing with God is Joyful, Easy, and Relaxing some of the time and definitely satisfying all of the time. When I feel Joyful, I AM One with God within my life.

Into Love, Success, and Abundance
When I Accept All That Is Now Here

The more I experience Joy, Ease, and Relaxation in my life, the more I support and experience Love, Success, and Abundance in my life. The best way to experience more Love, Success, and Abundance is through fuelling the Universal machine with my Feelings of Joy, Ease, and Relaxation.

Feelings of Joy, Ease, and Relaxation are encouraged by planting seeds of each in my daily life. Whenever I discover that I feel sad, frustrated or anxious, I Consciously look at and accept those Feelings and then I imagine the happiest thought I can think about the particular situation I am experiencing and then I can act as if it is so. The happiest thought I can imagine Uplifts and Encourages Joy and Potential in my life.

Joy, Ease, and Relaxation allow me to Be One with God and to accept what is Now Here. Accepting what is Now Here is Joyful, Easy, and Relaxing when I let go of what I imagine I need and realize that God's Gift in this situation takes me where I desire to go in the biggest scheme of things and is Chosen through my deepest heartfelt most secret beliefs.

Right Now is the Only moment of Creation I have access to. I Choose whether I AM in-tension or In-Joy. When I AM in-tension, I am tense and my present Vibrations order for me more experiences of tense Vibrations. Only I can Choose to believe in the illusions or my dreams.

When I AM In-Joy, my Choice is Being in-joy, no matter what the experience. From my Feelings of Joy, Ease, and Relaxation I support and experience Love, Success, and Abundance Always in All Ways.

I AM FEELINGS

Right Now is the Only moment of Creation
I have access to.
I Choose whether
I AM in-tension
or
In-Joy.

I AM Words

God Can Do Anything
God Can Do Anything through me
The Words I speak express my clarity of God
The world I experience
is a result of my Words of God
God's Word Manifests through
my Subconscious Mind
Which holds my
deepest heartfelt most secret beliefs about God
The reality I see and the dreams
I imagine are accepted
as equal within my Subconscious Mind
I program my Subconscious Mind
Always in All Ways
with Words of God

I AM Words

I AM WORDS

My Words convey to God all the things I desire to experience in life. My Words are so powerful that they provide me with the life I AM Living Now Here.

God Can Do Anything
God Can Do Anything through me

With all of my words I ask God and God provides. All my Words: the Happy, sad, frustrated, Abundant, Caring, hateful, Compassionate, judgmental, Blessing, unconscious, and Conscious Words are fulfilled by God through me. I ask (with my Words) and I receive.

God can do anything and God does everything in my experience through me. All of my Thoughts, Feelings, and Words place my order with God and Create my experience of Love, Life, and God. God can only do for me what God can do through me.

When I look at my Words, I see what I have been asking for in my life. When I talk about other people, places, and things as well as myself I AM Claiming those experiences for myself. When I curse, I am cursed. When I Bless, I AM Blessed. It is always my Choice of Words.

The Words I speak express my clarity of God
The world I experience is a result of
my Words of God

Absolutely everything in life is God. The concept of the devil is only a convenient way to deny my responsibility in my life. To claim that the devil made me do something, is to Choose to deny my responsibility. To claim that someone else is the devil denies my ability to help Create positive change in my experience of the world.

All the Words I speak express my clarity of God or my denial of God. There is nothing else. My Words can speak of separation, fear, failure, and lack of abundance or Unity, Love, Success, and Abundance.

The world I experience is a result of my Words of God. When I look at the world I am experiencing I discover the Words I AM speaking on a regular basis.

God's Word Manifests through my Subconscious Mind which holds my deepest heartfelt, most secret beliefs about God

All of my Words can Be spoken unconsciously or Consciously. My unconscious Words come forth when I experience separation from God. When I AM filled with depression, anger, and fear my Subconscious Mind is automatically activated and takes over my Conscious thoughts, feelings, words, and actions.

My subconscious mind is made up of my deepest heartfelt most secret beliefs about Love, Life, and God. These beliefs are Chosen Consciously in my past, usually during great emotional experiences. When a similar emotional experience comes up in the present, my subconscious Choices from my past are activated in the present until they are changed by me Consciously.

These subconscious Choices protected me in my past. However many Choices I made in my past, I would make differently if I experienced them for the first time today. When my Words in the present promote separation from Love, Life, and God, they are operating from my ego and through my subconscious. All my Words either promote fear and separation or they promote Love and Unity. My Words allow me to recognise and heal any separation I Choose from God.

The reality I see and the dreams I imagine are accepted as equal within my Subconscious Mind

My subconscious mind can be programmed through my imagination. My subconscious mind accepts both physical reality, as well as, imagined reality as one and the same. Something in the physical world is perceived in my Mind and Being. Something imagined is perceived in my Mind and Being. I can Choose to believe what I see in my reality or believe what I imagine is my reality. My subconscious mind accepts them as equal.

I program my Subconscious Mind Always in All Ways with Words of God

Every Word I speak programs my subconscious mind. If a group of Words are repeated consistently my subconscious mind eventually Accepts them as reality. Since I AM always at Choice I can Choose to use Words of God that promote my Unity with All of Love, Life, and God. I Choose Words of God. It is my Choice. I make my Choice for All of Love, Life, and God.

I AM WORDS

I AM Actions

All of my Actions express Who I AM
I AM the Source of my Abundance
I AM in-tension or Intension
I AM the Source of my Love
I AM Happy and Peaceful
I AM Easy and Relaxed
I Claim everything I Love
I Exclaim everything I Love
I AM Joyous Laughter
I AM Humbly Gracious
I AM Confidently Nervous

I AM Actions

All of my Actions express Who I AM

Who I AM is the sum of all of my Thoughts, Feelings, Words, and Actions. They combine to express Who I AM. My deepest heartfelt most secret beliefs about life and Who I AM is what I AM expressing in each and every moment. I just look at Who I AM and I know what I truly believe.

Do I believe in Love, Success, and Abundance? Do I believe in fear, failure, and lack of Abundance? Do I believe in war, murder, and evil? Do I believe in Peace, Healing, and Unconditional Love? Do I believe in conniving children, needy neighbours, and corrupt community members? Do I believe in cute children, nice neighbours, and compassionate community members? I Choose everything I believe. All of my Thoughts, Feelings, Words, and Actions Manifest Who I AM.

I AM the Source of my Abundance

My Actions are a result of my Thoughts, Feelings, and Words. My Thoughts, and Feelings inform my Words and Create my Actions. My Thoughts, Feelings, are the power within my Words and Actions.

I AM the Source of my Abundance. I AM the Source of absolutely everything in my experience. Absolutely everything in my experience allows me to Choose separation from God or Unity with God. When my experiences take me away from where I desire to go in life, I have only to change my Thoughts, Feelings, Words, and Actions to change my experiences.

I AM in-tension or Intention

My Consciousness Creates my consequences. My consequences and my Actions result from my level of

Consciousness. I AM either in-tension or Intention. My Intention within my consciousness Creates my experiences. When my Intention within my consciousness is in-tension, the consequences that result are also in-tension. When my Intention within my Consciousness is In-Joy, the consequences that result are In-Joy.

All of my Actions are a barometer displaying my deepest heartfelt most secret Intentions. My Core Beliefs set up my Creation Vibration which Attracts my experiences. My Intentions Create my consequences. Sometimes my consequences are my Conscious actions in a situation. Other times my consequences are my unconscious reactions in a situation. Either way my consequences match my beliefs about the reality (or illusions) before me.

I AM the Source of my Love

I AM the Source of absolutely everything I experience. Until I Choose to Accept my Responsibility in my life, I can believe that other people, places, and things affect my life. Other people, places, and things come into my life, however I make the Choices as to what impacts my life always in all ways. Nothing can impact my life, unless and until I Choose that experience through my thoughts and feelings.

I AM the Source of my Love. Love is all there is in Life. My being in-tension Creates my experience of lack of Love in my Life. My being in-joy Creates my experience of Love in my Life. It is always my Choice whether I AM in-tension or In-Joy. I Choose everything I experience.

I AM Happy and Peaceful

When I Choose to Be Happy and Peaceful in my experience, when I Intend for my experience to Be Happy and Peaceful, my Core Intentions set my Creation Vibration which Attracts my experiences of Happiness and Peace.

My Actions can also Create my Intentions. When I AM in-tension I can Choose to Act Happy and Peacefully in the face of tension.

When I Choose to Act as if I AM Happy and Peaceful my Thoughts, Feelings, and Words are accepted by my subconscious as my Intentions.

My subconscious accepts my view of reality whether it is experienced or imagined. When I Act as if, I Choose my imagination to be my view of reality. When I first Choose to Act as if, my entire experience will challenge my chosen view of reality until it becomes my reality over just Acting as if.

I AM Easy and Relaxed

The Power to Succeed in my life is ready and waiting for me to Consciously Choose to Succeed. All I need to Access this Power in my life is to make a Conscious Choice. The Choice I make need only be in an easy and relaxed manner. When my Intention it to Succeed, I have fully committed to my Success. It is my Choice and my Choice alone that puts me on the path to my Success. When my thoughts of Success match up with my feelings of Joy, I know that I AM Connected with God/Life/Energy through my Creation Vibration.

I Claim everything I Love

When I Intend Success, my ego (emotionally guided opinions) erratically screams my fears in all types of ways attempting to stop me from Choosing God over Choosing my ego.

Only I can Claim Love. Only I can Claim Power. Only I can Claim Abundance, Success, Radiant Health and Beauty, Peace, Pleasure, Dreams, and the Good Life. Only I can Claim God.

I Believe in God/Life/Energy. God is All That Is. Since God is All That Is, there is nothing working against me ever. My ego fosters beliefs in the power of anything other than God. Since God is All That Is, everything works for me and my benefit once I Claim my Power and Connect with God.

I Exclaim everything I Love

When I Claim my Belief in Only God, I also Exclaim my belief in Only God to myself. I need only exclaim it to myself, for my outer world matches my inner world. When I Claim and Exclaim my Belief in Only God, my world manifests Powerfully.

Until I commit fully to the Power of God Only, I allow my beliefs in anything other than God to deny my Power Centre. I AM Responsible for everything in my life. I Choose all of my Thoughts, Feelings, Words, and Actions that I experience, and everything I experience is a result of my Choices. I Ask and I Receive. I Believe in Only God.

I AM Joyous Laughter
I AM Humbly Gracious
I AM Confidently Nervous

When I AM Joyous Laughter, I AM in touch with God. Through me, God is bubbling Joyous feelings that come forth in peels of Laughter that lift everyone's spirits. When I Feel Connected with God, my laughter is infectious and natural.

I AM in touch with the Actions of God when I AM Humbly Gracious. I alone can do nothing. God can do everything. God is the Source and Supply of All Abundance. Abundance is All That Is. Abundant lack is still Abundance. I AM Humbly Gracious for All of God's Actions in my life.

I AM Confidently Nervous. God does everything through me. I AM Confident in God's ability. I Claim God's Power. There is nothing I can be without Claiming it first. God is Powerful. I Believe in God.

Everything that Manifests in my life is Manifested by God through me. God is All Powerful, I AM Nervous anticipation as I fully Align myself with God's Power.

God is All. I AM One within God. God is All within me.

My Intentions and their Actions set my Creation Vibration which Attracts my experiences.

I AM ACTIONS

I AM Heart

Joy is my compass
Love is my guide
Compassion is my presence
Nurturing is my mind
Blessing is my mouth
Listening is my ear
Sharing is my time
Cherishing is my life
Praising is my touch
Generous is my Love
Open is my Heart

I AM Heart

I AM HEART

I AM where I AM because I Choose it using my individualized Mind. I can Change my life by getting out of my Mind that Creates it. When I AM out of my Mind, I get into the space between my thoughts. The space between my thoughts is the access point to my Heart. My Heart is the pathway through which God Gives Ongoing Direction in my life.

When I AM in my Mind, I Believe that I am the source and supply in my life. When I AM in my Heart, I Know that God is the Source and Supply to absolutely everything in my life. When I AM Heart, I listen to everything the Universe shares with me through all the people, places, and things in my experience, and I access more through the way I Feel in my Heart.

Joy is my compass

When I AM in my Mind, I imagine that things go the way I Choose. When things go differently, I get sad, frustrated, or anxious. Over a long period of time, these feelings become depression, anger, and fear. These are the pathways of my ego (emotionally guided opinions) that are found only in a human mind. The human mind focuses on the things without me.

My Heart focuses on the things within me. When I AM in my Heart, I Choose Joy as my compass. When Joy is my compass, I AM Heart. When I AM Heart, I proceed from Joy and follow Joy and produce Joy. Joy is All That Is when I AM centred in my Heart. When I feel Joy I AM One with God in my life. Everything in my life is easily and effortlessly on track when I feel Joyful.

Love is my guide

God Giving Ongoing Direction in my life is Joyful. God is Kindness. God is Humble. When I AM in the Heart of the moment of Now, I AM Now Here. When I AM Now Here, I AM No Where else. When Love is my guide, I Choose what Love would do Now always in all ways.

Love is All That Is. Success is All That Is. Abundance is All That Is. When I imagine something else present in my life, I AM imagining from my mind. Anything other than Love is perceived within my mind. My Heart is Only Love.

Compassion is my presence

When I AM Mind, I AM thinking, hoping, wishing, and trying. When I AM Mind, I can Choose to embody any presence. When I AM Heart, I AM Heart. When I AM Heart, I AM Loving.

In my life, I can Only Be one thing at a time. I AM either Being Compassion or I AM thinking about Being Compassion. Being is a state I Choose. I Choose Being Compassion.

Nurturing is my mind

When I AM Heart, my Joy, Love, and Compassion Nurtures my Whole Heart, Mind, and Being. When I AM Whole and Complete, my Whole Heart, Mind, and Being operates in One Direction. That One Direction is God Giving Ongoing Direction.

My Heart Nurtures my entire Heart, Mind, and Being. When I AM Whole and Complete, God within me Gives One Direction: LOVE All That Is with All my Heart, Mind, and Being.

Blessing is my mouth

When I Feel Nurtured in my Heart, Mind, and Being, all of my Thoughts, Feelings, Words, and Actions Give One Direction: Love All That Is with All my Heart, Mind, and Being.

There are many ways to shower my Love upon others and myself. My Words are Love Expressed. I Choose Blessing Words. All the Words I use are the Words that come back to me multiplied.

Listening is my ear

I have one mouth and two ears so that I can listen twice as much as I speak. I listen to my own Words to Be Aware that my Words consistently place my order with God. My Words access God's Limitless Potential and Declare my experience into Being.

I listen to the Words of others. The Words of others are reminders from God about Who and What I AM and Consciously Choose to Be. Other people only Choose their life experience. Only I Choose my life experience. When I listen in my experience I AM Heart. I AM Joy, Love, Compassion, Nurturing, Blessing, Listening, Sharing, Cherishing, Praising, Generous, and Open.

Sharing is my time

When I Share my time, energy, and resources with others, others share their time, energy, and resources with me. I Share my personal expressions of God within me through all my Thoughts, Feelings, Words, and Actions.

Whatever I Choose to Share I experience that very thing as well. When I Share frustration, sadness, or anxiety, they are shared with me. When I Share Love, Success, and Abundance, they are also Shared with me.

In every moment Now Here, I Share Who and What I AM with All That Is. All That Is Shares Who and What I AM with me. Sharing is an Action I do all the time. Everything I AM Now Here is Shared with All That Is.

Cherishing is my life

When I AM Centred in my Heart, I Cherish All That Is. Everything in my experience brings me to the fullest expression of Who and What I AM. I Cherish All That Is, and All That Is Cherishes me.

All of Life is God Giving One Direction: Love All That Is

with all of my Heart, Mind, and Being. Since God is All, I AM One within God and God is All within me. Since there is Only One in the Universe, All That Is Loves Me and Cherishes me in return.

Praising is my touch

All of my Thoughts, Feelings, Words, and Actions touch All That Is. My individualized Being within God is interconnected with absolutely everything in existence.

I AM THE One within my experience of God/Life/Energy with the power to access All That Is and touch everyone in my experience. When I AM Heart my touch praises All That Is.

Generous is my Love

When I AM Heart, my Love is endless for my Love is the Love of God. When I Love Unconditionally, I Love because I AM Love and I Love All That Is.

Only in my mind can I Choose to Love conditionally. Only my mind can separate One thing from another. In my Heart All Is One. In my Heart my Love is Generous and Flows to All That Is.

Open is my Heart

I can Choose to close my Heart with Choices of my mind. My Heart will continue to Choose to Open my mind to new possibilities. The more I follow my Heart, the more my mind opens. This is a Conscious Choice I make in my journey.

I AM HEART

*Only in my mind can I Choose to Love
conditionally. Only my mind can separate One thing
from another. In my Heart All Is One.*

I AM Mind

I Love Everything
I Enjoy Everything
I Share Everything
I AM Everything
I Experience Everything
when
I lust after nothing
I require nothing
I expect nothing
I want nothing
I need nothing

I AM Mind

I AM MIND

I AM the captain of my ship. My ship is my Life. My Mind is my Captain. My Captain is in control of my life. When I use my Mind unconsciously, I sometimes run my ship aground resulting in costly repairs, or into icebergs resulting in needless deaths, or my ship ends up in Australia when I imagined I was going to Alaska.

When I use my Mind Consciously, I keep my ship in tip top shape, I make deliveries on time, and I upgrade my ship through my Choices.

My Conscious Mind is my Captain. God gives me Free Will to Choose any path I desire to follow in life. With every order my Captain makes to the crew of my ship, my Captain also makes requests to the crew of the entire Universe.

My Subconscious Mind is my Crew. My Subconscious Mind takes orders without questions and puts them into motion. My Subconscious Mind is also called by some: the Universe, God, Mother Nature, Higher Self, or the Soul.

The power my Captain is capable of accessing is Limitless, is Infinite, is Everything, is All That Is, is God/Life/Energy. Whatever I Believe with all my Heart, Mind, and Being, I can Achieve. My Free Will Allows me to Choose anything and Achieve anything I Believe.

What I Choose is up to me. The sooner I Choose to Go with the Joyful direction Life is suggesting I follow, the sooner I Accept all the Love, Success, and Abundance God is Manifesting on my behalf. I can Choose what shows up as the next step to All of my Dreams or fight it. Until I Choose Life's Gifts, I fight Life's Gifts.

I Love Everything

Absolutely everything in my life brings me one step closer to Unity with God and to Unity with my Love, Success, and Abundance. No matter what appears to be, everything is a stepping stone to my dreams. The quicker I Choose to Love Everything Now Here, the quicker I Unify with God/Life/Energy and I AM

Successful.

Loving everything that is Now Here is easy when I see the step that obviously leads towards my Success. When I Joyfully Love whatever is Now Here as my next step to my dreams, I Joyfully Allow Success to Manifest as well.

I Enjoy Everything

I Choose what I experience. I Choose Being In-Joy over being in-tension or being in-pain. It is always my Choice. When I Choose to Enjoy what is Now Here. I also access the point of Connection with God, which is Only Now Here. My Joy indicates my Connection with God.

I Share Everything

I Love, Enjoy, and Share everything in my experience and it keeps the flow of everything in my life. Life is Change. When I try to stop the Flow of one part of my Life, I Succeed in slowing the flow of my whole life. When I Flow with All of Life, All of Life Flows with me. I Give what I Live. I Share Love and Love is Shared with me. Everything I Share comes back to me as commanded by the Captain of my Ship.

I AM Everything

Everything in life is a mirror of Who and What I AM. I AM That I AM. Absolutely everything in my experience is a reflection of the screen within my Mind. Life's Illusions Change when I Change the way I look at them with my Mind. My Imagination is a powerful pathway I have access to.

There are some people who see death and destruction and everything they touch becomes dead and destroyed. There are others who see Gold Dust in the air and everything they touch is blessed with Abundance. The Only difference between these groups of people is their Thoughts. I Consciously use these Mirrors in my life to Choose my Connection with Thoughts that Uplift and Encourage the Joy and Potential in others and myself because I AM Everything. I AM All That Is. I AM God.

J Experience Everything

I Experience everything from the Mind set that I Love, Enjoy, and Share in my life. When I AM the Conscious Captain of my Ship, I Experience everything from a place of Humble Gratitude. My Humble Gratitude Allows me to see past the illusions of Life and into the Heart, Mind, and Being of my experience as I Choose and Live the Loving, Successful, and Abundant Life of my dreams.

when

J lust after nothing

J require nothing

J expect nothing

J want nothing

J need nothing

The mind of my ego (emotionally guided opinions) proliferates every idea that imagines I am separate from All That Is. The illusion of separation is just an illusion. God is All That Is.

The universe is made up primarily of space. The illusion of life is that everything manifested in space seems to make up the Universe, but the Universe is primarily made up of empty space. Even things that appear to be solid, when viewed at microscopic levels are actually full of empty space. All this empty space is God/Life/Energy. God is absolutely everything or rather God is

Absolutely Nothing (No Thing).

When my mind is caught up in what it is not, it is Choosing to experience what is not by my Choice alone. When I Lust after, require, expect, want, or need something, I AM Choosing to focus on what is Not instead of what is Nothing.

I AM Unified with All That Is. I AM Nothing. When I AM Nothing, I lust after, require, expect, want, and need absolutely No Thing.

As the Captain of my Ship, I Choose All I wish to foster and experience. I Choose to Love, Enjoy, Share, Experience, and Be everything when I lust after, require, expect, want, and need No Thing. When I need nothing, I AM No Thing. I AM God/Life/Energy.

I AM MIND

When I need nothing,
I AM nothing.

I AM
God/ Life/ Energy.

I AM Being

I AM Choosing everything I AM Being
When I AM Sad, I AM Choosing to BE
When I AM Wise, I AM Choosing to BE
When I AM Joyful, I AM Choosing to BE
When I AM Angry, I AM Choosing to BE
When I AM Loving, I AM Choosing to BE
When I AM Happy, I AM Choosing to BE
When I AM Fearful, I AM Choosing to BE
When I AM Successful, I AM Choosing to BE
When I AM Abundant, I AM Choosing to BE
I AM Choosing absolutely everything

I AM Being

I AM BEING

I AM Choosing everything I AM Being

In every moment Now Here, I AM Being something. I Choose everything I desire to Be. I Choose and God Supplies. This is the way I AM Creating My Own Experience. My thoughts, feelings, words, and actions set my Creation Vibration which Attracts matching Vibrational experiences.

The Universe, Love, Life, God, or whatever else I call All That Is produces my personalized commands, like an intelligent self-aware impersonal computer. The Computer of God takes my commands (no matter what they are) and produces and sends them to me in physical forms.

All of my Thoughts, Feelings, Words, and Actions make up my commands to The Computer of God, which The Computer of God manifests and inturn programs my command centre. This is a self-programming system, unless and until I Consciously Choose my states of Being.

When I AM Sad, I AM Choosing to BE

When I AM Wise, I AM Choosing to BE

When I AM Joyful, I AM Choosing to BE

When I AM Angry, I AM Choosing to BE

When I AM Loving, I AM Choosing to BE

When I AM Happy, I AM Choosing to BE

When I AM Fearful, I AM Choosing to BE

When I AM Successful, I AM Choosing to BE

When I AM Abundant, I AM Choosing to BE

In every moment Now Here, I AM Being something. Everything I AM experiencing, I AM Being, and I AM Choosing. Unless and until I recognise that my Choices of Being Create my Experiences of Being, I AM Being out of the loop. When I recognise that every moment of Now is a Moment of Creation, I Consciously Choose my State of Being.

What AM I Choosing to Be Now Here? Whatever I AM experiencing is also what I AM Being through my Thoughts, Feelings, Words, and Actions.

When I AM Angry, I AM Choosing to Be. When I AM Angry, I AM Choosing to send my Anger commands to The Computer of God. God allows me to Choose. God is the Source and Supply of everything I Choose. No matter what I Choose to Be. No questions asked. I Ask and I Receive. What AM I asking for Now Here?

When I AM in Conscious control of my Thoughts, Feelings, Words, and Actions, I AM also in Conscious control of my ability to Create my experience and I realise that I Chose every experience that is Now Here allowing me to Consciously Choose my State of Being.

I AM Choosing absolutely everything I AM Being

Free will has been described as my ability to Choose where I desire to go. Free will is my ability to Choose where I go with God. I can imagine that I do it all, yet unless and until I Choose to go with God, I go without God. It is always my choice.

I AM BEING

Free will has been described as my ability
to Choose where I desire to go.

Free will is my ability to Choose where
I go with God.

I can imagine that I do it all, yet unless and until
I Choose to go with God, I go without God.

It is always my choice.

I AM Experience

The Past is an illusion
The Future is a dream
The Present is a Choice
What time is it for me Now Here?
AM I hoping, believing, knowing, or Being?
AM I Loving, Successful, and Abundant?
I meditate to Feel God's Love, Success, and
Abundance within me, so God can
provide them without me
What gives me the most Joy
and Serves others Now Here?
That is God's Directions to me Now Here
What experience is Now Here?

I AM Experience

I AM EXPERIENCE

Whatever is Now Here is Only God. God is All That Is. God is All There Is. There is Nothing else because God is Nothing.

The Past is an illusion
The Future is a dream
The Present is a Choice
What time is it for me Now Here?

The past is an illusion. The past comes into the present moment forms of my experience. Every person, place, and thing Now Here, comes from past Thoughts, Feelings, Words, and Actions. All of my experiences come from my past Thoughts, Feelings, Words, and Actions.

All of these forms and experiences are illusions in which I can imbue my present Thoughts, Feelings, Words, and Actions to continue to Create them or to Change them. I Choose the illusions of life or I Choose God. It is always my Choice.

The future is a dream. The present moment provides me with urges to Create future dreams. Some of these urges are subtle forms and experiences, others are overt.

Future dreams give me a direction to aim towards, yet they are illusory too. To arrive at future dreams, I have to make present Choices that set my Creation Vibration towards the Manifestation of my dreams.

The present is a Choice. Each and every moment, I AM presented with an experience that allows me to Choose. Each Choice I make either moves me toward my dreams or away from them. The way to Consciously access where my present Choices take me is by Being One with God/Life/Energy. I AM One with God/Life/Energy when I feel Joyful.

What time is it for me Now Here? This simple question puts The Computer of God in motion to answer. The answer I receive comes through the forms and experiences presented within my life.

For example, lets say that my present thoughts and feelings encourage me to move toward my personal dream. I know my future dream of where I desire to go. I also know that I desire to Go with God in my journey. I ask myself, what time is it for me Now Here in that journey? The time for me Now Here in that journey is to make good feelings my goal over any forms. God takes care of everything else to get me from where I AM Now Here to my future dream. As my journey continues and evolves, I still only need to know where I AM going and what time it is for me Now Here? When I feel Joyful, I AM Creating my own Success with God.

$\mathcal{AM}$ $\mathcal{I}$ hoping, believing, knowing, or Being?

There are four levels of Creation ranging from particularly slow to instantaneous. I liken this journey of Creation to embarking on a trip from New York to Los Angeles.

Creation Time from N.Y to L.A.
(New York to Los Angeles)
(New Yearnings to Love Always)
Hoping equals riding a bike
Believing equals driving a car
Knowing equals taking a plane
Being equals instantaneous manifestation

These four levels of Creation get me from where I AM to where I desire to Be and they do so at different rates. There are no unrealistic dreams in the Mind of God. There are only unrealistic time lines in the mind of humans.

I can Hope something is going to happen. I can believe something is going to happen. I can Know something is going to happen. I can Be the thing I desire to happen. When I align with God, my dreams happen instantaneously.

When I align with human thoughts, feelings, words, and

actions, my dreams take whatever amount of time seems humanly possible. From a human perspective, reaching the Success of my future dreams is a lot like getting my dream train in motion. From a human perspective I imagine I am the desire that starts the engine on my dream train, while the caboose of the train is the final Manifestation.

I am in charge of getting my train from New Yearnings to Love Always, yet many times I imagine that I have to know each and every step of the journey in order to get from where I AM to where I desire to Be. Every new idea I attach to my dream is similar to attaching another train car onto my dream train. The more I think about my future dream, the more train cars I add to my train. All of a sudden my train becomes an incredible mass that is very slow to get to full speed.

God is the track that takes my dream train to my dreams. When I Ask for, Align with, Allow, and Accept Joy as my feeling of Choice I AM Making progress easily and effectively toward my Success. In my past, I have got off of my train just as it was starting to move or as it was very near approaching top speed towards my particular dreams.

God is Everything. God is the track, and the train engine and the caboose, God is All. God is the front and the back, the up and the down, the here and the there, and most importantly New Yearnings and Love Always wrapped into One. God is my One and Only Choice.

AM I Loving, Successful, and Abundant?

When I AM aligned with God, my New Yearnings and Love Always are a gift wrapped in One package, I AM Loving, Successful, and Abundant always in all ways. I use my mind as a Conscious Captain to Choose to BE Love, Success, and Abundance Now Here.

No matter what appears to Be in my experience, All That Is asks me to Choose to be the Grandest Feeling of God I can imagine. God always Chooses to Be Love, Success, and Abundance because there is Nothing else. God/Life/Energy

Encourages Joy and Potential always in all ways.

I meditate to Feel God's Love, Success, and Abundance within me, so God can provide them without me

I foster my growth within God by Choosing God within me. I meditate and Access the Feeling of God to Manifest God fully as my life. As within, so without. Until I go within, I go without. Free Will occurs when I decide to utilise the Gifts of God. When I decide to Feel and Actualise God's Love, Success, and Abundance within me on a regular basis, God can provide them without me on a regular basis. What AM I Choosing to foster Now Here?

What gives me the most Joy and Serves others Now Here? That is God's Directions to me Now Here What experience is Now Here?

Whatever brings me the most Joy and Serves others in this moment is God's Direction in my life. Every experience Now Here is calling me to provide myself Joy and Serve others. When I combine these two purposes I AM One with God in my experience. When I feel Joyful, I AM Creating My Own Success.

I AM EXPERIENCE

I foster my growth within God by
Choosing God within me.

I meditate and Access the Feeling of God
to Manifest God fully as my life.

As within, so without.

Until I go within, I go without.

I AM Success

Success is the journey to Being God Fully
I Give myself Only what I can Successfully Receive
I Enjoy people, places, and things for
my Enjoyment of them
I Enjoy No Where other than Now Here
Now Here is Successful Feedback
Now Here is Success
Success is assured in my journey to Being God Fully
God constantly says "Yes" to all of my dreams
I Only need to be Now Here to realise
that I AM Nothing, just like God

I AM Success

I AM SUCCESS

I AM God. I AM God in my life experience. I Choose everything in my life experience through all of my Thoughts, Feelings, Words, and Actions. My Success is supplied by God. I AM God in my life, and no other person's life experience.

Success is the journey to Being God Fully

My Success develops from my Choices. I Choose to Be God fully in all my experiences. When I AM Full of God, my journey is God Fully and I AM Successful.

I Give myself Only what I can Successfully Receive

As God in my life, I give myself Only what I can Successfully Receive. Prior to my full Awareness that I AM Captain of my life, I received many things without Knowing where they came from. Sometimes I imagined that I provided them. Now I know God is the Only Source and Supply.

I Enjoy people, places, and things for my Enjoyment of them

Whatever I AM, I continue to Be. I Enjoy people, places, and things and they continue to Be in my life for the Enjoyment of them. When I expect people, places, and things to Be in my life, then I AM expecting them and they never arrive. What I Enjoy, I experience Joyfully. What I expect, I hold myself in expectation.

I Enjoy No Where other than Now Here

When I AM in the Now I AM No Where else. I Enjoy what

is Now Here and I Choose to be No Where else. I Right Now Consciously set my Creation Vibration to energize my dreams, and I Consciously Choose to Attract my dreams. No matter what appears before me, there is a way.

Now Here is Successful Feedback
Now Here is Success

What some call failure is really Successful Feedback. Successful Feedback is a gift that I can Access easily. My Joyous feelings are my Successful feedback in the moment. When I feel anything which denies my Joy and Potential, I know I also deny my Potential Success. When I Allow my Joy, I AM Powerfully Allowing my Potential Success.

Success is assured in my journey to Being God Fully
God constantly says "Yes" to all of my dreams
I Only need to be Now Here to realise
that I AM Nothing, just like God

When I focus of being, doing, or having a particular form of Success, I desire something. When I desire something, I believe in the illusions of life as my source and supply.

When I focus on Being, Doing, or Having Nothing, I AM being like God in my life. When I Align with all of God's Love, Success, and Abundance, I experience my dreams of Love, Success, and Abundance as God/Life/Energy Manifests through my Choices.

I AM SUCCESS

When I Allow my Joy,
I AM Powerfully
Allowing my Potential Success.

I AM Lasting Freedom

I AM Physical Freedom
I AM Mental Freedom
I AM Emotional Freedom
I AM Spiritual Freedom
I AM Time Freedom
I AM Financial Freedom
I AM Relationship Freedom
I AM Loving Freedom
I AM Dream Freedom
I AM Choice Freedom
I AM God's Freedom

I AM Lasting Freedom

I AM LASTING FREEDOM

God provides absolutely everything in my life. I Consciously Choose God to provide my particular pathway to Success. I Consciously Choose God to provide me with Lasting Freedom. I define Lasting Freedom as being a combination of God in these forms and experiences in my life.

I AM Physical Freedom

God provides my life in physical form and experience. I Choose God as my Radiant Health and Beauty. I use my physical form to express and Create God fully in my physical experience. This brings me Joy and I Share it with others and myself.

I AM Mental Freedom

God provides me with my Free Will. I AM able to Choose anything I desire to experience in my life and God provides it for me. I use my Free Will mentally to Choose God as my Source and Supply in all of my life. My Choice to use my Free Will is also expressed in my personal talents. I use my talents to express and Create God fully in my mental experience.

I AM Emotional Freedom

God provides me with my ability to Feel in my experience. I am able to Choose to fully Feel all that Love, Life, and God have to offer me through God's Gifts to me. I use my emotional freedom to express and experience absolutely all emotions available within the human experience. I also use God's Gift to Choose the emotions I wish to foster in my experience by recognising that my Joyful Choices Create my Joyful experiences. When I Consciously Choose my better feeling experiences, I promote emotional freedom for others and myself.

I AM Spiritual Freedom

God provides me (and All That Is) with the ability to Choose from infinite paths to reach God. There are as many paths to God as there are people. Right Now there are almost seven Billion paths with God, not including all the paths of animals, plants, and other life forms. My Journey to God is varied and various and wonderful. God Manifests my experiences to match my Thoughts, Feelings, Words, and Actions. I use my Choices to Glorify God and God Glorifies my experience as a result.

I AM Time Freedom

God provides me with my life and all the time that makes up my life. God allows me to view time in anyway I Choose. I can imagine that I have little time to accomplish the dreams I envision. I can also Choose to Know that everything I could ever dream about at the deepest heartfelt, most secret levels comes to me always in all ways in the right ways and at the right time for my Lasting Success. When I live with a feeling of time freedom, my presence reflects onto others and back onto myself as God's Timelessness.

I AM Financial Freedom

God is Love, Success, and Abundance. Even Abundant lack is still Abundance. God provides me with a life of financial freedom. I AM Free to use my finances in any way I Choose. I can use my finances foolishly or build my financial freedom with them. It is always my Choice. No matter what I Choose, God provides me with whatever I Choose. I can Choose Abundant lack or Abundance and God provides for me. With my Abundance I Freely Share with others and I Tithe regularly. God is the Source and Supply of my Good and through my example my financial freedom exemplifies God's Gifts to me.

I AM Relationship Freedom

God is All That Is. Absolutely everything in existence is experienced in relationship to everything else. I Choose God as the Source and Supply of all my relationships, from the impersonal to the most intimate. In my relationships, I Choose to foster God and God's Gifts and I Bless others and myself as God Blesses me.

I AM Loving Freedom

God is Love. God within me Gives Ongoing Direction: LOVE All That Is with All my Heart, Mind, and Being. Love, Life, and God are One and the same. Love, like Life, like God is the One thing that is without end. I can give Love endlessly and it is instantly supplied. When I access and give love constantly then I AM God Fully and this benefits All That Is.

I AM Dream Freedom

God has provided me with a unique dream. My purpose, my dreams, and my talents are God's Gifts to me. All That Is glorifies me, when I access my purpose, dreams, or talents to glorify Love, Life, and God, This is a humble thought and experience. This direction is not filled and formed through my ego (emotionally guided opinions). This direction is Formed and Filled through God (Goodness Oneness Demonstrated). I Thank God for my dreams and God Manifests the dreams I Choose.

I AM Choice Freedom

God provides me with Freedom in my Choices. This has been called Free Will. Free Will had been described as my ability to Choose where I desire to go. Free Choice or Free Will is my ability to Choose where I go with God. I can imagine I do it all, yet unless and until I Choose to Go with God, I go without God. It is always my Choice.

I AM God's Freedom

God provides me with everything. God's Freedom is my freedom when I Choose to go with God. Before I AM Free, I Can Choose to go without or I Choose to Go with God. Right Now I AM Free and I Go with God Always in All Ways. This is the Only True Lasting Freedom.

I AM LASTING FREEDOM

Affirmations for my Success

Towards my personal Success there have been times when I Chose my ego (emotionally guided opinions) and doubted my Unity with God and my dreams.

Whenever I discover that I Right Now doubt something, I Consciously release my emotionally guided opinions and Consciously Access the Natural State of The Universe.

The Natural State of The Universe is Love, Success, and Abundance. This is obvious since the Universe continues to exist. If the opposite were true, the Natural State of the Universe would be hate, failure, and lack which would result in the ultimate demise of The Universe. That is Nothing like the Loving, Successful, and Abundant Universe I live in.

The Affirmations on the following pages are examples of some of the Loving, Successful, and Abundant reminders I have Created in my Journey to my Oneness with God and my successful realisation of my dreams.

I use my Mind to Be the Conscious Captain of my Life. I use my Conscious Mind to reprogram my deepest heartfelt most secret beliefs about life, especially when I am unaware of what they may be. I may not be Consciously Aware of what my deepest heartfelt most secret beliefs are, yet they manifest as my life experiences unless and until I Choose new beliefs.

I reprogram my beliefs using affirmations that affirm what I know to be true about my experience. God is the Source and Supply in my experience. I Choose to Unify with God so that my Success Manifests.

The following are 12 success beliefs I Consciously Choose that access the reality I AM, to achieve the Love, Success, and Abundance of my dreams by Choosing God and Love always in all ways.

#1

God is my Source and Supply. I Consciously Connect with God many times daily to align with God's Power and my dreams within God.

#2

With God, everything I attempt, I achieve in an easy and relaxed manner, in healthy and positive ways for the good of all concerned, or I receive my good in even better forms than I originally envisioned.

#3

I AM Unique. My Purpose in my Life is provided by God and is different from everyone else's purpose. I AM supported by God and my purpose contributes to All That Is

#4

God's Love, Success, and Abundance is Limitless. There is enough for everyone. Everything I require to achieve my dreams awaits my request and acceptance.

#5

God is the Only Source, Supply, and Support. Anything contrary in my life experience reminds me to Align with, Allow, and Accept God's Power within me.

#6

God imbues my entire heart, mind, and being with my individual talents and qualifications to achieve my dreams. I have a purpose and God Supports and Supplies everything I require to reach my dreams Always in All Ways.

#7

My dreams are assured with God as my Creator.
The time required to achieve my dreams is something
God has figured out in order for me to accept my
dreams only when I can sustain them and
they provide me with Lasting Success.

#8

My dreams are guaranteed with God. The dreams
I AM destined to Successfully Create in my
lifetime only need me to support their
direction a bit each day through my
Joyful Thoughts, Feelings,
Words, and Actions.

#9

God can accomplish anything. I can accomplish
anything when I Align with and
Access God's Power.

#10

Failure is only feedback on my Success journey.
All feedback ensures that particular pitfalls are
identified and changed so that I Completely achieve
my Lasting Success.

#11

I AM Grateful for the Power of God in my life.
Thank You God for my Life of
Lasting Success and Freedom.

#12

Life is set up for everyone to win.
When I feel good I AM letting my
Successful dreams joyfully in.

ABOUT THE AUTHOR

Barry Thomas Bechta is an artist, author, and film maker whose work centers around the concepts of Unconditional Love. Barry knew he wanted to write from a very young age and was encouraged with his artistic skills and only began writing full time in his thirties. He wrote his first book, *I AM Creating My Own Experience* as a personal journal to choose connection with God/Life/Energy. He has since written 17 inspirational spiritual books.

Barry loves to hear from people whom have connected with his writing and used it as a tool to improve their lives. If you would like to write him about your personal experiences as a result of reading any of his books, Barry encourages you to do so.

You can also get a Free Digital Copy of *I AM Creating My Own Experience - The Creation Vibration* from his main website:

www.unconditionallovebooks.com

Unconditional Love Books Titles of Related Interest
by Barry Thomas Bechta

I AM Creating My Own Experience
978-0-9813485-5-1
I AM Creating My Own Answers
978-0-9686835-1-4
I AM Creating My Own Dreams
978-0-9686835-2-1
I AM Creating My Own Relationships
978-0-9686835-3-8
I AM Creating My Own Abundance
978-0-9686835-4-5
I AM Creating My Own Success
978-0-9686835-5-2
I AM Creating My Own Happiness
978-0-9686835-6-9
I AM Creating My Own Experience - The Creation Vibration
978-0-9686835-7-6
I AM Creating My Own Experience - To Manifest Money
978-0-9686835-8-3
I AM Creating My Own Experience - 369 Conscious Days
978-0-9686835-9-0
Loving Oneness
978-0-9813485-0-6
Trust Life
978-0-9813485-1-3
I AM Creating My Own Financial Freedom - The Story
978-0-9813485-2-0
I AM Creating My Own Financial Freedom - The Lessons
978-0-9813485-3-7
Laughing Star's Guide to Laughter, Life, Love, and God
978-0-9813485-4-4

All of the above are books are available through your local
bookstore, or they may be ordered as digital downloads at
www.unconditionallovebooks.com

Barry Thomas Bechta is available for interviews, special events, workshops, and lectures that redefine, guide, and inspire everyone's connection to the Creative Power within themselves. To arrange author interviews, special events, workshops, or lectures, please contact:

UNCONDITIONAL
LOVE BOOKS

Unconditional Love Books
Box # 610 - 2527 Pine St.,
Vancouver, BC, Canada V6J 3E8

info@unconditionallovebooks.com

www.unconditionallovebooks.com

For additional copies of Barry's books, products, and services please contact your local book seller. Many products and services are Only available to order directly from the publisher as eProducts on the website.

Thanks for your purchase and Remember to Consciously Create your Life.

Right Now is the Only Moment of Creation

Enjoy it Fully!